Fish-it

Published by:
Pickard Communication
Unit 10-11 Riverside Park
Sheffield S2 4BB

Produced By: Chris Keeling

C000163623

ISBN: 1-905278-07-1

ACKNOWLEDGMENTS

I would like to thank the following for their
help in producing this guide:

Gary Mackender for art direction and cover design.

Michael Liversidge for print preparation.

Scott Roberts for advert design.

Jim Steele for venue information.

Barbara Clifton and Barry Mallett of the Boston & District Angling Association.

Colin Parker of the Lincoln & District Angling Association.

Billy Clarke Fishing Tackle for information useful in researching venues.

Thank you to all fishery owners who kindly provided information

and to those that gave permission to use

images from their websites.

Pickard Communication
Unit 10-11 Riverside Park, Sheaf Gardens
Sheffield, S2 4BB.

C O N T E N T S

W E L C O M E

Welcome to **Fish-it** a guide to coarse fishing in the
Lincolnshire area. This guide is aimed at the angler, like
myself who loves trying new fishing locations.

I wanted to produce a book that gave a good idea of
what a fishing venue has to offer before setting out on
sometimes a lengthy journey, only to be disappointed
when you reach your destination.

There is plenty of information along with photos of most
venues, so hopefully you will find the ideal water to suit
your method of fishing.

Lincolnshire is a big county and there are many more
venues that I haven't been able to include in this guide.
New fishing lakes are opening all the time, and with the
well hidden and un-advertised ponds there is possibly
enough to produce another guide.

If you have details of a venue and you would like it
included in a future publication, please fill in the form at
the back of this guide.

I hope you will find "Fish-it" Lincolnshire a useful guide
to trying different places to fish.

Chris Keeling

ABOUT THIS GUIDE

To help you locate a fishery, the venues have been arranged in alphabetical order and split into three sections, fisheries, drains and rivers. There approximate location has been indicated on the map overleaf.

Blue Section   Fisheries

Brown Section   Drains

Green Section   Rivers

Each page contains details of a fishery, with information on the following:

Ticket Price: All day ticket costs plus details on OAPs, disabled and junior concessions.

Directions: Usually from the nearest city or town, or from the closest motorway junction.

Description: A brief outline of what the fishery looks like plus details on features such as islands, depths and the best places to fish.

Types of Fish: List of species present, many with estimated weights.

Rules/Bans: The restrictions set by the fishery on type of baits, hooks etc.

Number of Lakes: The number of waters available to fish at the venue.

Facilities: What is available at each location i.e. cafe.

Telephone: The number of either the owner, angling club secretary or match organiser.

Blood Knot

This knot can be used to join two lines together, start by overlapping the ends of the two lines.

Twist one end round the other line four times and pass it between the two lines.

Do the same with the other end of line, making sure the previous step does not come undone.

Before pulling tight wet the knot to lubricate this also make it hold better. Trim off the two ends.

Half Blood Knot

Used mainly for joining hook to line.

Thread the end of your line through the eye of your hook.

Pass the free end underneath the line and bring it back over the line to form a loop.

Continue to loop the free end over the line about four times.

Pass the loose end between the eye of the hook and the first loop.

Pull on the loose end to tighten. Trim the line.

Double Overhand loop

This knot is used to create a loop at the end of a line. Also known as the surgeon's loop.

To begin, double the end of the line back against itself.

Tie an overhand knot in the doubled line.

The doubled end should then be tucked through the loop again.

Pull the knot as tight as possible and trim of the end.

Water Knot

This knot can also be known as the surgeon's knot. It is useful for joining a lighter hook line to your mainline

Hold the ends of the two lines alongside each other so that they overlap by about six inches.

Take hold of the two lines and make a wide loop.

Holding the two lines together. Pass the ends of the line through the loop four times.

Pull the lines tightly so that the loop makes a knot. Trim the two ends.

S P E C I E S
most commonly found in the Lincolnshire area.

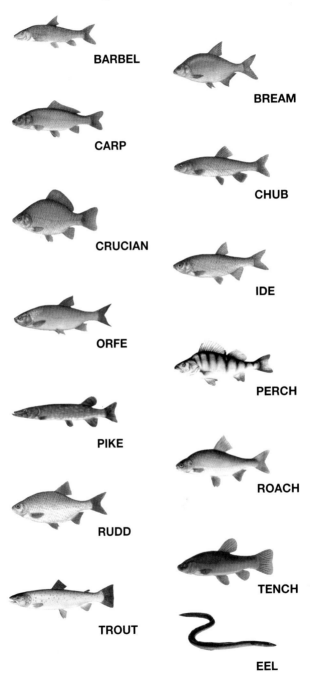

BARBEL

BREAM

CARP

CHUB

CRUCIAN

IDE

ORFE

PERCH

PIKE

ROACH

RUDD

TENCH

TROUT

EEL

S Y M B O L S

 Camping

 Caravan Site

 Drinks

 Disabled Access

 Toilets

 Food

 Parking

 Location of a fishery on the map

 Location of a river on the map

 Location of a drain on the map

To help you find the nearest place to get tackle and bait, you will find a list of fishing tackle shops in Lincolnshire on page 84.

I have tried to ensure the accuracy of this guide but things do change very quickly so if you know of any inaccuracies or any fisheries I have not included I would be grateful if you could fill out and return the form at the back of the guide or visit my website: **www.fish-it.co.uk** Lastly if you have or know of a fishery, pond or small lake for sale I know someone who would be very interested.

A.D.H Fisheries
Stain Lane, Strubby, Alford.

Ticket Price: Day tickets £5.00.

Directions: From Mablethorpe head towards Alford on the A1104. At Maltby le Marsh turn right. After 2 miles you will reach Strubby. Stain Lane is on your left.

Description: This fishery offers a peaceful days fishing, with no shops or cafes to distract you from this natural unspoiled fishery. The lake is well stocked and cared for. Target the margins for the regular bites.

Types of Fish: Carp, roach, perch, bream and tench

Rules/Bans: All fish to be returned to lake. No litter to be left. No carp to be put in keep nets.
Barbless hooks only.
No line, discarded hooks or floats to be left on bank sides or parking areas.

Number of Lakes: One

Facilities: Car parking, toilet.

Telephone: 01507 450236

Alvingham fisheries
Lock Road, Louth.

Ticket Price: Day tickets £5.00. Senior citizens and children under 13 £3.50.

Directions: From Louth head east towards Keddington. Go through Alvingham till you reach the canal bridge. Turn down a track at the side of the canal, follow it to the end where you will find the fishery.

Description: There are two well stocked ponds to chose from at Alvingham. The larger one has 22 pegs with an island running the full length with plenty of reed beds to target. The other smaller pond has only 15 pegs.
This is a excellent fishery with many features to target.

Types of Fish: Carp, golden orfe, tench, roach, rudd.

Rules/Bans: Barbless hooks only. No keepnets.
Baits allowed: Corn, pellet, paste, maggot, caster, worms and meat + ground bait in small quantities.

Number of Lakes: Two

Facilities: Ample car parking, toilets.

Telephone: 01507 328271

Ashby Park
West Ashby, Horncastle.

Ticket Price: Day ticket £5.00. Concessions to campers.

Directions: 1.5 miles north of Horncastle between the A158 & A153.

Description: There are seven lakes here at Ashby Park set in seventy acres of beautiful countryside. Parking is behind most pegs which makes it an excellent venue for the disabled angler. It is stocked on a regular basis and has many species.

Types of Fish: Top weights of carp 25lb 3oz, chub 5lb 8oz, roach and rudd 3lb 1oz, tench 9lb, bream 14lb 6oz, pike 28lb, perch 3lb 4oz.

Rules/Bans: Barbless hooks only. All children must be accompanied by an adult. No carp or large fish to be kept in keepnets.

Number of Lakes: Seven

Facilities: Parking, toilets, bait sold on site, camping & caravan site.

Telephone: 01507 527966

Bainside Fishing Lake
Kirkby on Bain, Woodhall Spa.

Ticket Price: Day ticket £4.00

Directions: From Horncastle take the A153 heading towards Coningsby. After about five miles turn right to Kirkby on Bain. Look for signs for the fishery.

Description: This fishery is set at the side of the River Bain and is around two acres in size. The long island strip that runs the full length of the lake is packed with features to target. The lake contains many species including some very nice grass carp up to the mid twentys. Plenty of tench can be caught using sweetcorn or luncheon meat. Float fishing is the popular method on this lake.

Types of Fish: Carp, tench, crucian, rudd, roach and bream

Rules/Bans: No boilies. No ground bait.
No keepnets. Barbless hooks only.

Number of Lakes: One

Facilities: Cafe, car parking, toilets. Ideal for the disabled angler

Telephone: 01526 352050

13

Bain Valley Fisheries
North Road Farm, Tattershall Thorpe.

Ticket Price: Day Ticket £4.00

Directions: Located between
Coningsby and Woodhall Spa.
Just of the B1192.
Close to the Blue Bell pub.

Description: Sixty acres of water
spread over eight lakes.This fishery
has most species of fish to try for. Ideal for both the pole
fisherman fishing the margins, and the feeder method
angler fishing the deep waters in the middle.

Types of Fish: Carp, tench, crucian, ide, perch, bream,
roach, rudd, and trout.

Rules/Bans: No nuts. Barbless hooks only.
Keepnets allowed at present.

Number of Lakes: Eight

Facilities: Parking near all lakes.
Toilet provided.

Telephone: 07779 589210

Belvoir Lakes Fishery
AJS Fisheries, Hungerton, Grantham.

Ticket Price: Day tickets £6.00. Concessions £4.50. Season tickets £60.00. Concessions £40.00.

Directions: From Grantham take the A607 heading towards Melton Mowbray. When you reach Denton turn right and follow signs for Belvoir Castle.

Description: The two large lakes of around 12 acres hold a good selection of double figure carp and bream plus pike to 25lb. The small lake of approximately 1 acre has been developed to offer all ages and levels of angler the opportunity to catch a wide variety of fish. This lake is perfect for anyone wanting to catch large numbers of smaller fish.

Types of Fish: Carp to 30lbs, bream to 13lbs, tench to 8lbs, pike to 25lbs. Plenty of roach, rudd, perch and chub.

Rules/Bans: No keepnets on small lake. No litter.

Number of Lakes: Three   **Telephone:** 01476 870647

Facilities: Parking.

Blyton Ponds
Station Road, Blyton.

Ticket Price: Day tickets £4.00 (2 rods).

Directions: Situated approximately 20 miles north of Lincoln between Gainsborough and Scunthorpe.
Take the A631 from Gainsborough towards Grimsby, turn left just before Corringham village, signposted Blyton and Pilham. You will find the ponds about 2 miles on right near the railway bridge.

Description: The fishery consists of three ponds, Pond (A) has 15 pegs, Pond (B) has 12 pegs. These two ponds are connected by a narrow channel. Pond (C) which is only open to residents Monday to Friday, but open for general day ticket fishing at the weekend has 16 pegs. There is ample car parking spaces with good disabled access, most pegs are flat, and all are made of paving slabs.

Types of Fish: All three ponds are well stocked with a great variety of fish, including common carp, mirror carp, crucian carp, ghost carp, chub, barbel, golden and green tench, roach, rudd, perch, and bream.

Rules/Bans: No keepnets. No groundbait. No hemp or boilies. Under 14's must be accompanied by an adult. Barbless hooks only.

Number of Lakes: Three. Fourth pond under construction.

Facilities: Parking, cafe and tackle shop, toilets caravans welcome, accommodation available.

Telephone: 01427 628240

Brayford Pool
Lincoln.

Ticket Price: Free fishing.

Directions: Follow sign posts for Lincoln City Centre.

Description: Brayford Pool is the Marina at the meeting of the Fossdyke Canal and the River Witham. Excellent venue for winter fishing as the pool has a good head of roach and bream in the colder months. Anglers also come for the pike.

Types of Fish: Roach, bream, pike and perch.

Rules/Bans: No fishing from the boat moorings.

Number of Lakes: One

Facilities: Plenty of facilities in the city centre.

Telephone: 01522 521452

Brickyard Fishery
South Somercotes, Louth.

Ticket Price: Day ticket £5.00.

Directions: From Louth head east on the B1200. When you meet the A1031 turn left to North Somercotes. Continue through Saltfleet and turn left into Dwe's Lane. Turn right at the crossroads then next right into Millfield Road. The fishery is two hundred yards on your right.

Description: This four acre lake is set within farmland in a very rural part of Lincolnshire. The average depth is 7 feet and there is good access to all banks and ample pegs. The lake has good stocks of silver fish plus some large carp. Target the reed beds for the best results.

Types of Fish: Carp to 21lbs, bream to 7lbs, tench, roach, rudd and a few eels.

Rules/Bans: Night fishing is allowed. Barbless hooks only. All baits are excepted

Number of Lakes: One

Facilities: Car parking. Most pegs suitable for the disabled angler. Toilets. Caravan facilities.

Telephone: 01507 358331

9

Brookside Fisheries
North Scarle, Lincoln.

Ticket Price: Day ticket £4.00 one rod. £6.00 two rods.

Directions: Head out of Lincoln on the ring road (A46). At the Whisby junction turn right. Follow the road through Eagle Moor until you reach a village called Eagle. Turn right and you will find the fishery at the next junction.

Description: This one acre lake is surrounded by large hedges on two sides giving a quiet secluded feel. It is a mature well stocked lake containing carp which reach 27lbs. There are plenty of features to target, pole fishing close to the reed bed margins gave constant entertainment with some excellent roach and rudd.

Types of Fish: Carp running to 27lbs, tench, roach, rudd.

Rules/Bans: No ground bait. No Keepnets. Barbless hooks only.

Number of Lakes: One

Facilities: Car parking, toilets, Caravan facilities available.

Telephone: 01522 778234

Butterswood Fisheries

Soff Lane, Southend, Goxhill.

Ticket Price: Day tickets £5.00, Concessions £3.00
Extra rods £1.00 (Open all year, dawn till dusk.)

Directions: Head towards Barton-upon-Humber on the A15.
Turn right at second crossroads onto College Road
(signposted East Halton). After about 2 miles take your
second left. Turn immediately to your right and go through
the green gates, the fishery is on the left.

Description: There are three lakes to try, the largest has 30
pegs and has an average depth of 6 feet. There are a few
double pegs which are very popular. The other two lakes
are smaller and have 16 and 17 pegs with some doubles.
Most pegs are suitable for the disabled.

Types of Fish: Carp to 25lb, tench and chub to 7lb, roach
and rudd to 2lb, perch to 3lb.

Rules/Bans: No keepnets. No groundbait. No boilies,
bloodworm, joker or hemp. No nuts of any kind. No dogs.
No Litter. No fishing from bridges.

Number of Lakes: Three

Facilities: Car park, toilets,
hot & cold drinks. Some baits are sold on site.

Telephone: 01469 530644

Caistor Fisheries
Brigg Rd, Caistor.

Ticket Price: Day tickets £4.50 (2 rods) Night fishing by arrangement 24hrs (2 rods)

Directions: Follow the A46 towards Caistor. At the top of the hill turn right and then immediately turn left into Caistor. Follow the road past the Talbot pub. Go past the sports ground and round a very sharp bend to the right. When you see a 50mph sign turn left into the fishery.

Description: Pond A is the smallest pond (10 pegs) and has been used as a rearing pond. It is well stocked with carp to 10lb, tench to 5lb, roach and rudd to a 1lb+, perch to 2lb. Pond B (20 pegs) has been producing several 100lb nets and is well stocked with plenty of double figure Carp. It has floodlights at pegs 19 and 4 for those wishing to night fish (by arrangement only). Pond C is well stocked with barbel, bream and chub. Whilst there are no giants in this pond, get them going and you are guaranteed tired arms by the end of the day. 30/40lb mixed bags are not uncommon.

Types of Fish: Carp, tench, rudd, roach, crucian, perch, barbel, bream, and chub.

Rules/Bans: No pets. Leave all litter in the bins provided. Keep all facilities clean and tidy. Keepnets are allowed please use the dip tanks. Barbless hooks only.

Number of Lakes: Three

Telephone: 01472 852032

Claxby Fishery
Market Rasen.

Ticket Price: Day tickets £5.00. Concessions and school children £4.00. Evening ticket (after 5pm) £4.00

Directions: Head north from Market Rasen on the A46. Turn right at Claxby Moor, then second right. Cross the railway line and you will find the ponds and car park on your left.

Description: The fishery consists of three ponds that are well stocked with a variety of fish. Both common and mirror carp reach 16lbs and are in excellent condition. The ponds are closed between the end of September and the 1st of February.

Types of Fish: Common and mirror carp, crucian carp, tench, bream, roach and rudd.

Rules/Bans: No night fishing. Barbless hooks only. No fish over 2lbs in keepnets.

Number of Lakes: Three

Facilities: Car park, toilets, disabled access

Telephone: 01673 828272

22

Dykes Cottage Ponds
Chapel Hill, Nr Coningsby.

Ticket Price: Day tickets £4.00, two rods £6.00.
Under 11yrs and OAPs £3.00.

Directions: From Coningsby head towards Sleaford on the A153. From Tattershall Bridge take the road to Chapel Hill which runs along the side of the River Witham. When you reach the Crown Inn turn left, follow the track to the fishery.

Description: Two ponds to chose from, both having an island in the middle and plenty of reed beds to target. Average depth of five feet. The carp which can reach into the low twentys in weight mainly patrol the islands. Plenty of silver fish and a few eels are present.

Types of Fish: Carp, tench, bream, roach, perch, crucian carp and eel.

Rules/Bans: No hemp. Barbless hooks only. No keepnets except in matches.

Number of Lakes: Two

Facilities: Car parking, pub near by, toilets.

Telephone: 01526 343315

East Halton Lake
East Halton

Ticket Price: Day tickets £4.00 adults.
£2.00 Concessions. (Pay at the bungalow after 8am)

Directions: Take the A180 from Grimsby and head towards Scunthorpe. Turn right after three miles onto the A160 at South Killingholme. Go straight through South and North Killingholme heading for East Halton. Cross over a railway line and shortly afterwards turn right into Marsh Lane. The lake is at the end of the lane.

Description: A 15 acre lake containing mixed coarse fish. Fifty-five pegs available on day tickets. This is mainly a roach rudd and perch fishery with some bream and tench present. A small amount of carp have been introduced but it's like trying to find a needle in a hay stack to catch one.

Types of Fish: Roach, perch, rudd, bream, tench and carp

Rules/Bans: Barbless hooks only.
Sensible use of ground bait. No litter.

Number of Lakes: One

Facilities: Car parking, male & female toilets

Telephone: 01469 540238

24

Fossdyke Canal
Between Lincoln and Saxilby.

Ticket Price: £2.50 on the bank. Annual tickets available.

Directions: The canal runs alongside the A57 lincoln to Saxilby road.

Description: This section of the canal is very popular not only for the pleasure angler but with club match organisers as well. At around 20 metres wide and 5 feet deep in the channel, it is ideal for most methods. Its the perfect pole venue with red maggot if you want good nets of roach and some large bream.

Types of Fish: Bream, roach, perch

Rules/Bans: Barbless hooks only.

Facilities: Car parking is not allowed on the roadside, but there are several lay-bys and car parks

Telephone: British Waterways Board
01827 252000

Goltho Lakes
Goltho, Nr Wragby, Market Rasen.

Ticket Price: Day ticket £3.00. Fishing from 7am till 8.30pm Open all year. Phone for seasonal time changes.

Directions: From Wragby take the A158 heading towards Lincoln. After one mile turn left signposted Goltho/Apley. Travel for another mile and you will find the lakes on your left.

Description: These very well kept waters consist of two lakes both with depths of around five to six feet. The first lake has 16 pegs, the second has 22 pegs. Both are stocked with a mixture of silver fish, but bream and tench are the dominant species.

Types of Fish: Carp running to 25lbs, bream to 8lbs, tench to 6lbs, plenty of roach, perch, rudd and chub.

Rules/Bans: No ground bait. No boilies, cat or dog food. Barbless hooks only. Nets to be dipped. No litter or noise

Number of Lakes: Two

Facilities: Car parking, toilets. Two pegs suitable for the disabled angler. Caravan and camping available but you need to book first.

Telephone: 01673 858671 or 01673 858358

17

Grange Park

Grange Park Leisure Complex, Messingham.

Ticket Price: Day tickets £4.00. Concessions £3.00.

Directions: Turn off the M180 at the Scunthorpe Junction 3 exit and travel along the M181 for two miles. Take the A18 signposted Ashby. Turn off onto the A159, follow this road to a crossroads. Turn right signposted East Butterwick, don't follow the Messingham sign. Grange Park is just past Messingham Sands fishery, on your left hand side.

Description: This single lake is around two acres in size and is part of the leisure facilities available. One side of the lake is next to the golf course which is not fishable. I spoke to a man from Rotherham who had been fishing from 5am with his son and between them had caught 40 good sized carp. Most methods work here with depths of 3-4 feet in the margins and nearing 20 feet in the middle

Types of Fish: Carp, roach, bream, and tench

Rules/Bans: No keepnets. Barbless hooks only. No groundbait. No litter.

Number of Lakes: One

Facilities: Car parking, toilets, disabled access, cafe, caravan hook ups.

Telephone: 01724 762851

Hall Farm Moat
Harpswell, Gainsborough.

Ticket Price: Day tickets £4.00. Children & OAPs £2.00. To be paid at farm house. Open all year.

Directions: Head out of Gainsborough on the A631. The farm is about 8 miles on your right. Turn in at the Hall Farm Nursery sign.

Description: This medieval moat is around 3/4 of an acre in size and about 5 feet deep. It is a very attractive and well sheltered spot. Not readily accessible for the disabled as there is a short walk on uneven grass land.

Types of Fish: Carp from 2lbs to 20lbs, good sized tench and lots of roach.

Rules/Bans: Barbless hooks only. No keepnets. Please use small quantities of ground bait. No night fishing.

Number of Lakes: One

Facilities: Car parking in farm yard.

Telephone: 01427 668412

Hatton Lake
Horncastle Rd, Hatton.

Ticket Price: Day tickets £4.00

Directions: Leave Lincoln on the A158 and head towards Wragby. The fishery is on the left of the main road (A158) between Wragby and Horncastle.

Description: This well kept small fishery has two islands to target plus many other features. It has 26 well spaced pegs with most being suitable for the disabled angler.

Types of Fish: Carp, tench, roach, rudd, perch and crucian

Rules/Bans: Barbless hooks only. No groundbait. No children under 14yrs unless with an adult.

Number of Lakes: One

Facilities: Car park and toilets.

Telephone: 01673 858682 (8am to 7pm)

Haven Fishing Pond
Nr Messingham, Scunthorpe.

Ticket Price: Day Ticket £5.00 Concessions £4.00

Directions: Head out of Scunthorpe on the Scooter bottom road, heading south to Scooter. The pond is half a mile on your left after crossing the M180 bridge.

Description: This single lake has many species including rainbow trout. The carp and tench are the dominant species with a good head of rudd and bream. The pond has an average depth of 7 feet and plenty of margins to target on one side. Meat or corn worked for me.

Types of Fish: Carp to around 11lb. Tench, rudd, crucian, chub, perch, bream and trout.

Rules/Bans: No keepnets. Barbless hooks only.
All litter must be removed.

Number of Lakes: One

Facilities: Car parking.

Telephone: 01724 762331

Haverholme Park
Ewerby, Sleaford.

Ticket Price: Day ticket £5.00. Evenings £4.00.

Directions: Head east out of Sleaford on the A17. At Kirkby la Thorpe turn left and go through the village. Turn next left heading to Ruskington. The lake is signposted on your left handside.

Description: This well known match lake has a track record of producing some great bags of around 150lbs. This two and a half acre lake has only 24 pegs with some excellent swims. Depths vary dramatically in this old clay pit, finding yourself at 13ft deep at only 20 yards out. I found the margins productive, targeting the reed beds and lilies.

Types of Fish: Carp, roach, tench to 5lbs, bream to 3lbs, perch, rudd and ide

Rules/Bans: Barbless hooks only.

Number of Lakes: One

Facilities: Car parking. Some pegs suitable for the disabled angler

Telephone: 01526 832125

22

Hill View Lakes
Hogsthorpe, Chapel St Leonards.

Ticket Price: Day tickets £5.00. £6.00 on the bank.
Tickets purchased from the cafe.

Directions: From Skegness, take the A52 heading towards
Mablethorpe. The fishery entrance is signposted on the left
before Hogsthorpe Village.

Description: This touring and static caravan park in
Hogsthorpe has three lakes, one of which is for site
residents only. With depths to around six feet the two acre
carp lake has carp to 25lbs. The much smaller lake (around
3/4 of an acre) also has some good carp to 20lbs along with
most other species of silver fish.

Types of Fish: Carp, tench, bream, roach, crucian and perch.

Rules/Bans: No keepnets. Barbless hooks only. Nets must
be dipped. No ground bait or feeders.

Number of Lakes: Three

Facilities: Car parking, toilets,
good access for the
disabled angler, cafe.

Telephone: 01754 872979

Hollands Park
Thorpe St Peter, Skegness.

Ticket Price: Day Tickets £3.50

Directions: From Boston head north on the A52 towards Skegness. Turn left at Wainfleet All Saints onto Boston Road. Continue through Wainfleet All Saints and take Spilsby Road to Thorpe St Peter (B1195). Turn right just as you reach the village. Take your next right into Wedland Lane and you will find the fishery on your left.

Description: Four nice ponds to choose from with plenty of space between the pegs. The fisherman I spoke to rated this venue very highly. Ideal for novices who want plenty of bites. Most were pole fishing and catching in the margins.

Types of Fish: Carp, bream, tench, roach, chub, rudd and perch

Rules/Bans: Barbless hooks only.
Sensible use of ground bait. No litter.

Number of Lakes: Four

Facilities: Car park, toilets, camping, touring caravans.

Telephone:
01754 880576

33

Homestead Park Lake
Washdyke Lane, Immingham.

Ticket Price: Day tickets £4.10

Directions: Take the M180 heading to Grimsby. Keep on the same road as it changes to the A180. Come off at Habrough and join the A160. Go straight over the next roundabout. After 1 mile turn onto the A1173. Turn right and after 300 yards turn right again into Washdyke Lane.
The lake is on your right just after the first bend in the road.

Description: Catches of 50lbs in the summer months are not uncommon, with carp to 20lb caught around the island. Large chub have also been caught, weighing in at 5lbs.
The reeds at one end are good to target but the weed at the shallow end can cause problems. There are 40 pegs with 4 concrete platforms suitable for the disabled angler.

Types of Fish: Bream, roach, perch, tench, rudd, carp and chub

Rules/Bans: No bloodworm. Barbless hooks only. Keepnets are allowed.

Number of Lakes: One

Facilities: Car parking, toilets, disabled pegs.

Telephone: 01469 574606

Horncastle Golf Lake
West Ashby, Horncastle.

Ticket Price: Day ticket £5.00

Directions: The lake is at the golf club. Look out for it on the left as you head towards Horncastle on the A158.

Types of Fish: Carp, tench, roach and perch

Rules/Bans: Barbless hooks only.

Number of Lakes: Two

Facilities: Parking, toilets, bar and food.

Telephone: 01507 526800

Mill Hill Lakes
Bratoft, Skegness.

Ticket Price: Day ticket £3.50. Extra rod £1.00

Directions: From the A158 at Burgh le Marsh. Take the Wainfleet road. At the junction with the B1195 turn right. Follow the road for about 500 yards and you will find the lakes on your right.

Description: Mill Hill has two lakes to chose from. The larger one has 22 pegs and does stock the bigger carp. The smaller one has 16 pegs and is shallower. Both lakes have a good selection of silver fish.

Types of Fish: Carp, rudd, tench, chub, perch and barbel.

Rules/Bans: No boilies, groundbait, or hemp. No fish over 2lb in keepnets. Barbless hooks only.

Number of Lakes: Two

Facilities: Car parking, toilets.

Telephone: 01754 810788

Kingfisher Lodge
Hibaldstow, Brigg.

Ticket Price: Day tickets £3.00 one rod. £4.00 two rods.

Directions: Leave the M180 at junction 4 and take the A15 to Lincoln. After 3 miles turn left to Hibaldstow. Turn right continuing on the B1206. Take your next left (Hibaldstow Bridge). After just under a mile turn left and you will find the fishery 300 metres on your right.

Description: This 3 acre fishing lake has 35 pegs many suitable for the disabled angler. The depth is between 3 and 8 feet. Parking behind each peg makes life very easy on the back, if like me you have to much tackle. This lake is stocked with quality fish of most species.

Types of Fish: Carp to over 24lbs, bream and tench to 6lbs, chub to 6lb, perch to 3lb, roach and rudd to 2lb.

Rules/Bans: No night fishing. No carp in nets. No groundbait except in feeder. Barbless hooks only

Number of Lakes: One

Facilities: Car parking, caravans welcome, toilets.

27

Telephone: 01652 652210

Lake Ross
West Pinchbeck, Spalding.

Ticket Price: Day tickets £6.00 (Dawn to Dusk)
£4.00 per evening (4pm to Dusk)

Directions: Lake Ross is easily located 2.5 miles west of
Spalding on the A151 to Bourne in the country village of
Pode Hole.

Description: The lake is set within a small family run caravan
park and is well stocked with a variety of course fish,
including some quality barbel. Access is available to all
banks with plenty of pegs and stages suitable for the
disabled angler.

Types of Fish: Carp, tench, roach, rudd, chub, and barbel.

Rules/Bans: Barbless hooks only. No floating baits.
Groundbait in open end feeder only. No boilies.

Number of Lakes: One

Facilities: Car parking, toilets, camping & caravan hook-ups

Telephone: 01775 761690

37

Lakeside Leisure
Trunch Lane, Chapel St Leonards.

Ticket Price: Day tickets £5.00. 2 rods £8.00

Directions: From Skegness take the A52 north. Go through Ingoldmells and turn right. Take your second right which is Trunch Lane. Continue to the sea wall and follow the tourist information signs to the lakes.

Description: Four lakes to chose from, starting with the Boating Lake that is 3.5 acres holding the larger carp up to 34lbs and reported catfish to 54lb. Kingfisher Lake has been stocked with trout which have to be returned. It also has carp to 8lb and a good head of silver fish. Horseshoe Lake has an island and reed beds to target carp again to 24lbs, plus some lovely tench. The last and smallest pond is the Golf Pond which is heavily stocked with most species including small barbel.

Types of Fish: Bream, barbel, carp, chub, golden orfe, rudd tench, perch, roach, trout

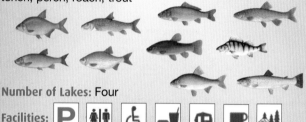

Number of Lakes: Four

Facilities:

Rules/Bans: No keepnets. Barbless hooks only.

29

Telephone: 01754 872631

Langdale Fisheries
Langworth, Nr Lincoln.

Ticket Price: Day tickets £5.00.
£6.00 on Friday's and weekends.

Directions: Take the A158 from Lincoln heading east. You will reach Langworth after a couple of miles. The fishery is on your left-hand side. Keep a look out for the fishery sign.

Description: This very attractive fishery has two ponds. Willow pond which is ideal for matches has plenty of tree lined margins to target the carp which reach 20lbs. Lily Lake has been established for 100 years and boasts over 200 doubles with the largest being approximately 38lbs. If you prefer something smaller there are plenty of bream and tench to around 9lbs.

Types of Fish: Tench, carp, bream, crucian carp, roach, rudd, perch, chub and a few pike

Rules/Bans: Barbless hooks only. No carp over 2lb to be kept in keepnets. No tiger nuts or any other type of nut as bait or groundbait. Under 16's must be accompanied by a responsible adult. Radios must be kept at a low volume.

Number of Lakes: Two

Facilities: Parking, toilets, caravan pitches, camping

Telephone: 01522 752414

39

Messingham Sands
Messingham, Nr Scunthorpe.

Ticket Price: Day tickets £5.00. Concessions + evening £4.00

Directions: Turn off the M180 at the Scunthorpe junction 3 exit and travel along the M181 for two miles. Take the A18 signposted Ashby. Turn off onto the A159, follow this road to a crossroads. Turn right signposted East Butterwick, don't follow the Messingham sign. You will find the fishery on your left hand side.

Description: With nine lakes this fishery is one of the biggest in the area. It has 6 match lakes and 3 day ticket lakes. The smaller match lakes have around 20 pegs which makes them ideal for club matches. These are not fishable on a day ticket basis. All lakes seem to be packed with fish as most people were catching including the young angler. The great plus point is to be able to park behind most pegs.

Types of Fish: Carp, rudd, roach, bream, chub, perch, tench, crucian carp.

Number of Lakes: Six match only, three day ticket lakes.

Rules/Bans: No bait bans but pellets have to be bought on site. No night fishing. Barbless hooks only. No keepnets except in matches.

Facilities: Good parking, shop, cafe, toilets,

Telephone: 01724 763647

Mill Road Lakes
Skegness.

Ticket Price: Day tickets £4.50. Extra rods £2.00.
OAPs and juniors £3.50. After 4pm £3.50.

Directions: From Horncastle head east on the A158. About 5 miles before Skegness you will reach Burgh le Marsh. Turn left to Addlethorpe. You will come across the fishery on you left hand side.

Description: This very attractive fishery consists of two ponds, both contain carp to 30lbs and tench to around 7lbs. The pegs are nicely spaced with most of them having a reed bed to the side where most people were targeting. These are not big ponds and do seem to suit the pole angler.

Types of Fish: Carp, tench, perch, rudd, bream, and roach.

Rules/Bans: Barbless hooks only. No ground bait. No boilies or nuts. Dogs to be kept on a lead at all times.

Number of Lakes: Two   **Telephone:** 01754 767586

Facilities: Car park, toilets, cafe.

33

41

Moon lake Fisheries
Bank Farm, Marsh Lane, Tattershall.

Ticket Price: Day tickets £5.00. After 5pm £4.00. Concessions £4.00. Match booking £5.00 each.

Directions: From Sleaford head north on the A153. Go through Billinghay. When you reach the centre of Tattershall turn left onto the B1192. The fishery is about 1 mile on your left hand side. Look out for the small 'brown fish' tourist information signs.

Description: Moon Lake is the largest of the five waters, it is two acres in size and 30 good pegs to fish from. Circular in shape with a small island in the middle ideal to target the many species available. The other waters are of canal type and are excellent for pole fishing.

Types of Fish: Carp, bream, tench, barbel, ide and chub.

Rules/Bans: Barbless hooks only. No braid. Ground bait by feeder or pole cup only. No keepnets except in matches.

Number of Lakes: Five

Facilities: Parking, toilets, disabled access.

34

Telephone: 01526 345377

42

North Kyme Pitts

(Lockeys) North Kyme.

Ticket Price: Day ticket £5.00. Concessions £4.00.

Directions: Take the A153 from Sleaford. Turn left over the river 300 yds before you reach North Kyme. Turn left again in approximately 500 yds. The fishery can be found at the 2nd farm on your right.

Description: These two heavily stocked Lakes are mainly for the lover of carp. Most carp are between 4 and 7lbs, but there are a few that reach 20lbs. The Match Lake does have plenty of silver fish to target as well as carp.

Types of Fish: Roach, rudd, perch, chub, carp, bream and crucian.

Rules/Bans: Barbless hooks only. No carp in keepnets.

Number of Lakes: Two

Facilities: Plenty of parking. Toilets

35

Telephone: 01526 860875

43

Oakhill Leisure
Norton Disney, Lincoln.

Ticket Price: Day tickets £6.00 (2 rods). £7.00 (3 rods) 24hrs £13.00

Directions: Conveniently situated off the A46 between Lincoln and Newark on Trent. Look for the signpost to Thurlby & Norton Disney.

Description: This mature 5 acre lake is able to accommodate 40 pegs approximately. Well shielded by bushes and trees the lake is fully stocked with carp, tench, rudd and bream. Most angler come for the carp, as there are quite a few that reach the 35lb mark.

Types of Fish: Carp to 35lbs, tench, rudd and bream.

Rules/Bans: Maximum of 3 rods per angler. No keepnets. No tiger nuts or peanuts.
Barbless hooks only. £1.00 off when camping on site

Number of Lakes: One

Facilities: Parking, toilets, camping, caravans welcome.

Telephone: 01522 868771

Oasis lakes
Warren Rd, North Somercotes, Louth.

Ticket Price: 16+yrs £5.00 per day for one rod. 11-15 yrs £4 per day for one rod and under 10yrs £3 per day for one rod. Concessions £3 per day for one rod. Additional rods are charged at an additional 50% of the appropriate day rate for your age. The Carp Lake is £5 per day for one rod regardless of age and a further 50% for additional rods.

Directions: Take the B1200 from Louth. At the A1031, turn left and follow the road to the village of North Somercotes. In the village, take the first right after the large caravan park, signposted Oasis Lakes.

Description: Three lakes to chose from, the largest called Carp Lake is 1.8 acres with an average depth of 9 feet. Double figure carp up to 38lbs and a massive one day record pleasure catch of 525lb. Slightly smaller is Roadside Lake which has mainly silver fish. Island Lake is just under an acre and is also the shallowest at 5 feet. This lake has most species and is more suitable for the younger angler.

Types of Fish: Tench, crucian carp, roach, rudd, perch, carp, barbel, chub, and bream.

Rules/Bans: Barbless hooks only. No trout pellets. No fish over 3lbs in keepnets. No spinning.

Number of Lakes: Three   **Telephone:** 01507 358488

Facilities: Car parking behind most pegs, tackle shop. Male and female toilets, cafe.

Oham Lakes
Maltby le Marsh, Alford.

Ticket Price: Day Ticket £5.00 (2 rods). Concessions £3.00

Directions: From Louth follow the signs for Mablethorpe on the A157. This will take you through several villages before you come into Maltby le Marsh. At the T-junction in Maltby turn left and the fishery entrance is a short way down the road on your left.

Description: The fishing is on three pools, one developed for younger angler where it's a fish ever few minutes and the other two holding everything from silver fish through barbel and chub to mirror and common carp to over 30lbs. This fishery has developed a lot over recent years and now has an excellent cafe and well stocked tackle shop

Types of Fish: Common, mirror, grass and leather carp. Bream, roach, rudd, tench, chub, barbel and crucian.

Rules/Bans: Barbless hooks only. No keepnets.

Number of Lakes: Three

Facilities: Ample parking, toilets, tackle shop, cafe, camping, caravan hook-up.

Telephone: 01507 450623

46

Orchard Park
Hubberts Bridge, Boston.

Ticket Price: Day tickets £5.00

Directions: Take the A52 from Grantham heading towards Boston. Turn left onto the B1192 at the Four Cross Roads Public House. The lake is two hundred yards on your left just after the bend in the road.

Description: Set within a holiday park this five acre lake attracts angler from all over the country. Maybe the four species of carp has something to do with it. There is a single island in the middle but this is some distance to target. Try the many reed beds that surround the lake for the tench and carp.

Types of Fish: Bream, rudd, roach, tench, perch and carp

Rules/Bans: Barbless hooks only, No keepnets.

Number of Lakes: One

Facilities: Car parking, toilets, disabled access, caravan and camping facilities.

39

Telephone: 01205 290328 / 290368

Pasture House Fisheries
Pasture Rd, Barton-Upon-Humber.

Ticket Price: Day tickets £5.00 one rod, £7.00 two rods
Night fishing by prior permission.

Directions: At junction 5 of the M180 head towards the
Humber Bridge on the A15. Turn left into Brigg Rd B1218.
Turn right onto the A1077. Left into Whitecross Street. Bear
left onto Pasture Road. The fishery is on your left hand side.

Description: Two great lakes to try. One at around 6 acres,
the other at an acre and a half. The Carp Lake with 21 pegs
and is nearly 9 ft deep with mirror, common and ghost carp
plus a lot of silver fish. Main Lake has a maximum depth of
20 feet with 46 pegs. A further 16 pegs can be found at the
south of the lake over a wooden bridge.

Types of Fish: Roach, rudd, carp, tench, crucian, bream,
barbel and ide

Rules/Bans: Barbless hooks only. Limited groundbait,
No fish over 6lbs in keepnets. No braid. Children under 12
must be accompanied by an adult.

Number of Lakes: Two   **Telephone:** 01652 636369

Facilities: Cafe, Disabled access, toilets.

48

Priory Lakes
Ruskington, Nr Sleaford.

Ticket Price: Day tickets £5.00

Directions: From Sleaford head north on the B1188. When you reach Ruskington turn right onto Station Road. Look out for the fishery on your right hand side.

Description: Priory lakes are made up of two similar sized waters of around 3.5 acres. Lake 1 has two islands to target and is well stocked with most species of coarse fish and has sixty well spaced pegs.
Lake 2 has four islands and is mainly a carp lake with again around sixty pegs. The carp can reach into double figures.

Types of Fish: Carp, crucian, tench, bream, rudd, roach, chub and perch.

Rules/Bans: Barbless hooks only. No keepnets except in matches. No boilies.

Number of Lakes: Two

Facilities: Secure parking, toilets

Telephone: 01526 834444

Rainwater Lake
Low Road, Skegness.

Ticket Price: Day tickets £5.00

Directions: From Boston head towards Skegness on the A52. Two miles after you pass the Wainfleet Bypass turn left at Lomax's Garage. The lake is 100 metres on the left.

Description: The prominent species in this well stocked lake are carp, rudd and tench with the biggest catch being a massive 29lb mirror carp. There are plenty of other silver fish present making this lake ideal for the novice and experienced angler. The pegs are well spaced out giving a feel of seclusion.

Types of Fish: Rudd, roach, bream, tench, perch, and carp.

Rules/Bans: Barbless hooks only. No keepnets.
No groundbait. No bloodworm or hemp.
Children under 14 must be accompanied by an adult.

Number of Lakes: One

Facilities: Car parking, toilets, Caravan facilities available.

Telephone: 01754 765783

Revesby Reservoir
Revesby.

Ticket Price: Day tickets £5.00. Concessions £4.00
7.30am till dusk Mon-Sat, Sunday matches only.
Open 16th June to 15th March.
The Wong Lake is open all year. £140 per year.

Directions: Just off the A155 on the B1183. One mile north
of Revesby. Entrance to lakes signposted Revesby reservoir.

Description: There are two lakes set in mature woodland.
The reservoir is 35 acres with over 40 fishable pegs. with a
depth of 5ft to 8ft. The second smaller lake is called The
Wong and is 4 acres in size. This is stocked mainly with
carp, but is for carp club members only. Both lakes have
some access suitable for the disabled angler.

Types of Fish: The reservoir has roach, bream, tench up to
12lbs. Some large perch and pike. Small head of carp up to
30lbs. The Wong has common mirror carp between 8lbs
and 24lbs.

Rules/Bans: No ground bait. No live baiting. No fixed leads
or tiger for the carp. Barbless hooks only. Nets to be
dipped. No night fishing. No dogs.

Number of Lakes: Two

Facilities: Two car parks. Toilets situated all around the
lakes, telephone for assistance and advice.

Telephone: 01507 568395 (office) 07778 955718 (mobile)

Roach Farm Park
Burgh Road, Skegness.

Ticket Price: Day ticket £4.00. Children under 14 yrs and OAPs £3.50. After 4.30pm £3.00 and £2.50

Directions: Situated on the main road it is easily found on the A158 between Skegness and Burgh Le Marsh. It is signposted from Burgh Le Marsh and you would have to pass Roach Farm Park in order to reach Skegness.

Description: There are plenty of pegs that are well spaced and a decent size, so more than one angler can fish off each. This is an added bonus for younger fishermen as it means they can sit next to dad in safety and learn how to catch those 20 pounders that he is always talking about.

Types of Fish: Currently stocked with roach, rudd, tench, bream, perch and chub also numerous species of carp including mirror, ghost, hybrid, common and leather.

Rules/Bans: Barbless hooks. Nets must be dipped. No carp or tench in keepnets. No ground bait, boilies or nut

Number of Lakes: Three

Facilities: Parking, tackle shop, toilets, caravan hook-up,

Telephone: 01754 898049

Rossways
Wyberton, Boston.

Ticket Price: Day tickets £5.00, Concessions £4.00

Directions: From Boston take the A16 heading towards Spalding. After 1 mile turn right at the roundabout into London Rd. You will find Rossways after half a mile on your right hand side.

Description: Rossways has two beautiful mature lakes. The main lake has 19 pegs with a depth of about 8 feet, which is where you will find the larger carp. The smaller lake has only 5 pegs with a depth of 4 feet. Both are well stocked with a variety of fish.

Types of Fish: Carp to 30lbs, bream, tench, roach, chub barbel, ide, golden orfe and perch.

Rules/Bans: No keepnets. Barbless hooks only. No Litter.

Number of Lakes: Two

Facilities: Car park, toilets,

Telephone: 01205 361643

Saltfleetby fisheries

Main Rd, Saltfleetby, Louth.

Ticket Price: Day ticket £5.00 one rod. £7.00 two rods Concessions £3.00.

Directions: The fishery is situated 6 miles east of Louth on the B1200. Between Louth and Mablethorpe.

Description: As you can see from the photo there are three ponds all of which are well stocked. The Main Lake is an old brick pit which is two acres and has a depth of between 4ft and 20ft. Island Pond is one and a half acres, Silver Pond is just under an acre, both these ponds are around 4ft deep.

Types of Fish: Bream 7lb, tench 7lb, carp to 25lb, rudd 3lb, crucian carp 2lb, roach 1 1/2lb, perch 3lb + eels 3lb.

Rules/Bans: Barbless hooks only. All nets to be dipped. Groundbait in feeder or pole cup only.
No large carp in keepnets.

Number of Lakes: Three

Facilities: Car parking, toilets, bait and tackle shop, food and drinks available, touring caravan site.

Telephone: 01507 338272

46

54

Skipworth Arms
Moortown, Nr Caistor.

Ticket Price: Day ticket £5.00. Dawn to Dusk

Directions: From Grimsby take the A46 heading towards Lincoln. When you reach Netherton follow the signs to Moortown. You will find the pub when you reach a railway crossing. Turn into the back car park and the lake is at the far end of the field.

Description: There is only the one small lake which has around 10 pegs. This new lake has changed ownership recently and is very well stocked with plenty of quality fish.

Types of Fish: Tench, rudd, carp, and crucian carp.

Rules/Bans: Barbless hooks only. Keepnet are allowed, max 6 hours. Standard rules and regs apply.

Number of Lakes: One

Facilities: Car parking. Public House is open for toilets, food and drinks.

47

Telephone: 01472 851770

South Cliff Farm Fishery
South Cliff Farm, Lincoln.

Ticket Price: Day ticket £4.00

Directions: From Lincoln drive north on the A15. The fishery is before you get to the A1500 on the left hand side just before the Lincoln Showground.

Description: This four acre nearly square lake has more to offer than it seems. The reed beds in one corner offered good pole fishing for carp reportedly in the twenties. With a depth of around 10 feet all over the lake you will come across more than just carp. There are large roach, rudd and bream reaching 6lb.

Types of Fish: Carp, tench, bream, roach, rudd, ide, and perch

Rules/Bans: No Keepnets. Barbless hooks only. No night fishing. No litter.

Number of Lakes: One

Facilities: Car parking

Telephone: 01522 730236

Sudbrook Pond
Ancaster, Grantham.

Ticket Price: Day ticket £4.00

Directions: Head out of Sleaford on the A153 towards Grantham. Straight on at the crossroads in Ancaster. Take the first turning on your right into Rookery Lane. After a row of small cottages you will find the fishery on your left.

Description: There's very little shelter around this lake, but a slight breeze didn't stop me from catching. This one acre lake which seemed bigger has an average depth of 7 feet. I fished close to the small island next to the roadside and caught plenty of small carp and roach. Try sweetcorn for the carp and tench. The trusty red maggot for the perch.

Types of Fish: Perch up to 2lbs, tench, carp, roach, bream.

Rules/Bans: No Keepnets. Barbless hooks only.

Number of Lakes: One

Facilities: Parking, adjoining caravan and camp site, disabled access.

Telephone: 01400 230388

49

Swanlake
Culvert Rd, Wainfleet, Skegness.

Ticket Price: Day tickets £5.00. Concessions £4.00
7am till dusk. March to November.

Directions: Signposted on the A52, between Boston and Skegness.

Description: There are two lakes to chose from. The largest is 2 acres and has been established for about fifty years. The other is in its first year and is about 1 acre. Depths vary in both with its deepest being 8 feet in the middle. Both are stocked with a variety of quality fish.

Types of Fish: Carp, tench, roach, rudd, barbel, perch and crucian

Rules/Bans: Barbless hooks only. No carp in nets. Handle fish with respect.

Number of Lakes: Two

Facilities: Car park and toilets.

Sycamore Lakes
Burgh le Marsh, Skegness.

Ticket Price: Day ticket £5.00 one rod. £9.00 two rods.
OAP's, Disabled, Under 16yrs £4.00 one rod.

Directions: From Skegness head west on the A158.
Sycamore Lakes are on your left just before you reach
Burgh le Marsh.

Description: There are four heavily stocked fishing lakes.
Three of them have carp over 25lb, tench, rudd, roach and
perch being the prominent species. Island Lake is a two
acre water with a depth of 5-6 feet with a deeper hole at the
north end. Specimen Lake is for carp and is popular for
ledgering with the majority being 12lb to 28lb. Roadside
Lake is one and a half acres and is 6ft in depth. This lake
also has many large fish. Lastly Woodland Lake. This is
known as the match lake and is slightly deeper with a small
central island and camping areas around it.

Types of Fish: Carp, tench, roach, perch, rudd.

Rules/Bans: No keepnets except in matches.
Barbless hooks only.

Number of Lakes: Four   **Telephone:** 01754 811411

Facilities: Cafe, tackle shop,
camping, caravans welcome, disabled toilets.

51

59

Tattershall Park

Tattershall Park Country Club, Tattershall.

Ticket Price: £6.00 Day ticket or £4.00 if booked with accommodation. £10 for 24 hours
£75.00 season ticket. £45.00 under 16's and over 65's
£30.00 for 7 day ticket
Concessions under 16's and over 65's £4.00 Day ticket.

Directions: From Sleaford take the A153 heading to Horncastle. Cross over the River Witham. When you reach Tattershall follow the signs to the park.

Description: There are four lakes at this venue, but only two are fishable by day ticket. Island Lake has some large specimen carp and a few big pike along with most other species. Rudd Lake has coincidentally plenty of rudd with good sized tench and bream. There is good disabled access to fish the lakes.

Types of Fish: Carp, tench, bream, rudd, perch, roach, pike, barbel and chub.

Rules/Bans: Barbless hooks only.

Number of Lakes: Two day ticket lakes

Facilities: Parking, toilets, cafe, caravan and camping

Telephone:
01526 348800

Tetford Country Cottages
Tetford, Horncastle.

Ticket Price: Full day from 7am until dusk, £5 adult, £3 for under for 16's. After 3pm until dusk £3 adult, £1 under 16's.

Directions: From Horncastle head east on the A158. Enter Tetford from Salmonby, turn right after the Cross Keys pub into South Road then first left into East Road. Pass the old sawmill on your left and continue around the bend. The entrance is 150 yards on the left just past Manor Farm house.

Description: The lake is 2.5 acres and an ideal water for the pleasure angler. It is well stocked with bream, tench, roach, rudd, perch and carp to 27lb. There are 34 pegs to chose from. Wheelchair access to two pegs is along a path and then a short distance over grass.

Types of Fish: Perch, carp, rudd, tench, bream and roach

Rules/Bans: Barbless hooks only. Night fishing is only available to residents. No keep nets after dusk. Rod limit of two. No fixed lead or fixed method feeder rigs.
Use unhooking mat for carp. Use all bait in moderation.
No fish over 2lb to be kept in a keepnet. No dogs.
Dispose of all rubbish including used shot/tackle and unwanted bait into the bins provided.

Number of Lakes: One   **Telephone:** 01507 533276

Facilities: Cafe shop, tackle store.

Tetney Lock (Louth canal)
North Cotes, Grimsby.

Ticket Price: Free

Directions: From the A16 Grimsby to Louth road. Take the A1038 heading to Tetney. From the crossroads in Tetney follows the sign to Tetney Lock. Travel for 2 miles past the large green oil tanks on your left hand side. Just before the bridge turn right opposite the red telephone kiosk. The lane is signposted The Wharf.

Description: This stretch of canal is run by Tetney Lock Angling Club. It is well known for its large pike in the winter months. Very popular with the local angler. This may have something to do with excellent food in the pub nearby.

Types of Fish: Roach, bream, carp, chub and pike.

Rules/Bans: No litter please.

Number of Lakes: One

Facilities: Parking on the roadside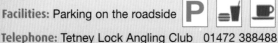

Telephone: Tetney Lock Angling Club   01472 388488

62

Trentside Fisheries
Burton upon Stather, Nr Scunthorpe.

Ticket Price: Day Tickets £5.00. Concessions £3.50.

Directions: From the Humber Bridge take the A1077 towards South Ferriby. Stay on this road until you reach a right turn signposted Thealby/Burton upon Stather (B1430).
At the Sheffield Arms pub take a right down Stather Road. Take first left off Stather Road, then next right towards the riverbank where you will find the fishery.

Description: This seven acre lake is set in a beautiful location on the banks of the River Trent. It has 37 platform pegs suitable for the disabled angler.
Match booking are taken. There are further ongoing developments which will make it even better.

Types of Fish: Tench, bream, rudd, roach, pike and carp to 30lbs.

Rules/Bans: No Keepnets. Barbless hooks only.

Number of Lakes: One

Facilities: Parking and toilets

Telephone: 01724 720325

West Lodge Lakes
Whisby, Lincoln.

Ticket Price: Day tickets £4.00 (one rod) £6.00 (two rods)

Directions: From Newark head towards Lincoln on the A46. Turn left just before the Pride of Lincoln pub staying on the A46 ring road. Turn left at the next roundabout. The lakes are a couple of hundred yards on your right. (Across the road from Whisby Garden Centre)

Description: This attractive but small venue is definitely worth a visit. I could see plenty of carp just under the surface. Use a pole and target the end of the island on the first pond. This worked for me and the chap from Nottingham who was fishing the other end of the island.

Types of Fish: Carp, tench, roach, perch and bream.

Rules/Bans: Barbless hooks only, Dip landing nets, No keepnets, No floating baits, No boilies, No litter.

Number of Lakes: Two

Facilities: toilets, parking, caravan hook up.

56

Telephone: 01522 681720

Whisby Garden Centre
Whisby, Lincoln.

Ticket Price: Day tickets £4.00. Concessions £3.50

Directions: From Newark head towards Lincoln on the A46. Turn left just before the Pride of Lincoln pub staying on the A46 ring road. You will find the fishery at the next junction on your left.

Description: This five acre site comprises of three lakes all of which are stocked the same. Most species are present but the mainly dominant one is the carp which reach an impressive 26lbs. There's plenty of good sized bream to around 7lbs. Most methods work; pole, waggler and feeder with maggot, meat or corn. The cafe is worth a try, they do an excellent breakfast.

Types of Fish: Bream, crucian, roach, ide, tench and carp.

Rules/Bans: Barbless hooks only, 1 pint of hemp allowed. Ground bait through feeder or pole cup only. No boilies. Night fishing by appointment. Keepnets only in matches.

Number of Lakes: Three

Facilities: Parking, cafe, toilets, disabled access.

Telephone: 01522 685395 Bailiff 07947 295779

57

Willowbank Fisheries
Station Rd, Kirton Lindsey.

Ticket Price: Day ticket £20.00, 24hrs £40.00, 48hrs £70.00
Membership £475 per year Mar 07- Feb 08

Directions: Leave the M180 at Junction 4. take the A15 south towards Lincoln. At Kirton Lindsey take the B1400.

Go over the railway bridge and you will find the fishery on your left opposite a garden centre.

Description: Willowbank specialise in "Specimen Fishing", mainly being carp and catfish. They have a wide range of fish in three lakes. The main lakes have many features such as Islands, margins and underwater features. The fishery is secure, tranquil and picturesque. There are also 7 smaller ponds mainly stocked with carp.

Types of Fish:
Very big carp, huge catfish.

Rules/Bans: Best bait for carp are: boilies, pellets, worms, maggots, bread and floater.
Catfish: live baits, liver, squid, spicy sausage and luncheon meat.

Number of Lakes: Ten

Facilities: There is a building on-site which has a shower, hot/cold water, toilet, TV, fridge/freezer, microwave and kettle. This is free of charge for the angler. Free use of wheelbarrows. Small Car Park.

Telephone: 01652 648452

Woodland Waters

Willoughby Rd, Ancaster, Grantham.

Ticket Price: Day ticket 5.00. Concessions £3.50.
Carp fishing £8.00 per day. 24hr ticket £20.00
Additional rods £2.00

Directions: From the south take the B6403. Just past
Colsterworth turn left at Ancaster crossroads. The waters
are 300yds on the right. From the north take the A17 to
Newark and join the B6403. At Ancaster crossroads turn
right and you will find the waters on your right after 300yds.

Description: The biggest of the five lakes at Woodland is
the Specimen Lake at over 14 acres, with an average
depth of 17ft. This lake has mainly carp , bream and pike.
The next largest is the match lake which is 7 acres
and averages 12 feet deep. There are also three smaller
lakes each with about 20 pegs. These are heavily stocked
with carp, roach, tench and rudd.

Types of Fish: Carp to 32lbs, tench to 11lbs, roach to 2lbs,
perch to 4lbs, pike to 31lbs, bream to 10lbs.
Plenty of crucian and rudd.

Rules/Bans: Barbless hooks only. No keepnets or
groundbait on small lakes

Number of Lakes: Five

Telephone: 01400 230888
or 07949 892392

Facilities: Full camping and caravan facilities. Disabled
toilets. Bar and restaurant.

Specimen Lake
(Dam End)
26lb Common

Woodlands Fishery
Ashby Rd, Spilsby.

Ticket Price: Day tickets £5.00. Second rod £2.00. Senior citizens and children £4.00. After 4pm £3.00.

Directions: Leave the A16 at the Spilsby junction. After half a mile turn left at the George Hotel into Ashby Road. Follow the road for 1 mile and turn left at the fishery entrance.

Description: Woodlands is a 5 lake complex with over 100 pegs, a few custom made for the wheelchair angler. Hawthorn Lake is the newest and largest at around 2 acres and has been heavily stocked with mirror and common carp, plus a mixture of silver fish and tench.

Types of Fish: Carp to 20lbs, crucian carp, tench, bream, rudd, roach and perch.

Rules/Bans: Barbless hooks only. No carp in keepnets or fish over 3lbs. No bloodworm, joker, dog or cat meat. No nuts or boilies. No trout pellets.

Number of Lakes: Five

Facilities: Ample car parking, flush toilets, tackle shop, hot & cold drinks

Telephone: 01790 754252 or 07767 304540

Woodthorpe Hall
Woodthorpe Hall Leisure Park, Nr Alford.

Ticket Price: Day tickets £4.50. Weekly per person £22.50. Family daily permit £7.00 one adult, one junior.

Directions: Woodthorpe Hall is situated just off the B1373 about 1.5 miles from Withern village and just over 3 miles from the market town of Alford.

Description: This very picturesque one acre lake is well stocked with tench, roach, rudd, orfe, carp and perch. Close by is the Country Inn which is set within the leisure park. The pegs are well spaced out and most have a reed bed to one side, so you can target the good sized tench which like the shade.

Types of Fish: Tench, roach, rudd, orfe, carp and perch.

Rules/Bans: No loose ground bait to be used except in a reasonable sized bait feeder or small cupping system. Boilies on the hook only. No hemp, or trout pellets to be used. Barbless hooks only. No carp over 3lb to be kept in keepnets. No night fishing allowed. Maximum of 2 rods per person. No litter to be left. No radios allowed. No baited gear may be left unattended. No children under the age of 12 allowed to fish un-supervised. All fish caught are to be returned.

Number of Lakes: One   **Telephone:** 01507 450294

Facilities:

Yaddlethorpe Ponds
Scooter Rd, Scunthorpe.

Ticket Price: £5 per peg. £5 per rod on the specimen lake. £4 Juveniles and OAP's. Night fishing £10 by arrangement.

Directions: Come out of Scunthorpe heading towards Scooter on the A159. You will find the ponds opposite Jewitt's Landscape and Building Materials, 3 miles from Scunthorpe town centre.

Description: Yaddlethorpe ponds is a truly beautiful fishery set in stunning surroundings. Of the 12 lakes on site, 7 are now open for fishing, the remaining 5 are currently being used as stock and breeding ponds. The Specimen Lake is where the 25lb carp can be caught along with plenty of tench and bream to 6lb. The Match Lake, Bathing Hole and Tench Pond are all heavily stocked with most species. If you like peace, quiet and beauty give it a try.

Types of Fish: Carp, tench, roach, perch, rudd, bream + pike

Rules/Bans: Keepnets allowed except in Specimen Lake. Bait bans. No nuts. Ground bait through pole pot or feeder. Strictly barbless hooks only.

Number of Lakes: Seven

Facilities: Parking, toilets, disabled access.

Telephone: 07775 683037

River Welland

From Spalding to Crowland Bridge.

Ticket Price: Day tickets £3.00 on the bank.
Free fishing on the stretch that goes through Spalding town centre.

Directions: From Peterborough head towards Eye. Take the A1073 sign posted Crowland. Turn left onto the B1166 and go through Crowland until you reach the bridge. Peg 1 starts at Spalding and reaches the 700s at Crowland Bridge.

Description: There are bream to double figures, tench to 7lb, roach average 2lb, carp, chub, pike to double figures and eels. Waggler, leger or groundbait feeder in the middle or beyond with red maggot or worm is best. Waggler or pole method with a maggot on the near shelf is ideal for the small roach. Eels show in summer months.

Types of Fish: Roach, tench, chub, pike, bream and eel

Rules/Bans: No bloodworm, joker or live baits.

Facilities: Plenty of parking at the riverside

63

Telephone: Peterborough & District AA on 01733 65159

Upper River Witham
From Lincoln to South Hykeham.

Ticket Price: L&DAA annual memberships are available from local tackle shops.
Adults £24.00. Disabled & OAPs £14.00.
Juniors (under 17) £7.00
Day tickets available at location. Adults £3.50
Concessions £2.50

Description: The upper River Witham has a growing reputation for specimen bream. There is also plenty of tench, perch and pike plus the excellent winter roach fishing. There are some platforms for the disabled, between Firth Rd and Coulson Rd.

Types of Fish: Bream, tench, perch, pike and roach.

Rules/Bans: No live fish, particle bait, bloodworm & joker.

Contact Details:
Frank Butcher
Chairman/Match Secretary
14 St Andrews Gardens
Lincoln LN6 7UQ
01522 534174

Contact Details:
Colin Parker
Secretary
4 Pottergate Close
Waddington
Lincoln LN5 9LY
01522 720777

River Trent

At North Clifton and Laughterton.

Ticket Price: L&DAA annual memberships are available from local tackle shops.
Adults £24.00. Disabled & OAPs £14.00.
Juniors (under 17) £7.00
Day tickets available at location. Adults £3.50
Concessions £2.50

Description: At North Clifton you can fish the tidal Trent, near the noted "Bridge Peg" that has yielded numerous good catches of chub. The venue holds bream, roach, skimmers, perch, carp and an increasing number of barbel.

Types of Fish: Bream, carp, perch, barbel and roach.

Rules/Bans: No live fish, particle bait, bloodworm & joker.

Contact Details:
Frank Butcher
Chairman/Match Secretary
14 St Andrews Gardens
Lincoln LN6 7UQ
01522 534174

Contact Details:
Colin Parker
Secretary
4 Pottergate Close
Waddington
Lincoln LN5 9LY
01522 720777

Annual Members of the Association can also fish waters of the **Witham & District Joint Anglers Federation** including **Fossdyke Canal** from Brayford Pool to Torksey Lock. **Sincil Drain**, The **River Witham** and a section of the **River Bain** near Coningsby. Also ponds at **Boultham Park**, **Starmers Pit** and **Brewery Farm Lakes**.

Information kindly supplied by
Lincoln & District Angling Association

River Till
Saxilby, Nr Lincoln.

Ticket Price: Day tickets on the bank £3.50.
Concessions £2.50

Directions: From Lincoln head west towards Saxilby on the A57. After 3 miles the road crosses the river. There is a car park next to the river.

Description: How the river is running decides the method to fish. If its flowing use a stick float, but in the summer months it can be very slow and I prefer to use a pole. The River Till is only 20 metres or so in width and looks more like the average drain than a river. Anglers were doing well feeding hemp. Try caster and maggot for the roach and perch.

Types of Fish: Perch, roach, bream, pike.

Rules/Bans: No Bloodworm.

Facilities: Car park near river.

Telephone: 01709 866333 or 01522 534174

River Ancholme
Brandy Wharf

Ticket Price: Day ticket £3.00 on the bank.

Directions: From Lincoln head north on the A15. About 5 miles after the Caenby junction, turn right onto the B1205 sign posted Waddingham. Continue through Waddingham until you reach the river. Cross the bridge and turn left.

Description: Fishes well all year round, but is popular in the winter months with anglers targeting the shoals of roach. Like a lot of rivers in Lincolnshire this section looks and has simular species as many drains in the area. I was lucky and landed some good sized bream and some hungry perch. This stretch is often used for matches and can be busy.

Types of Fish: Bream, roach, perch and pike

Rules/Bans: None

Facilities: Parking behind most pegs.

Telephone: 01652 635224

View from Hibaldstow Bridge

River Steeping
Wainfleet.

Ticket Price: Tickets on the bank £3.50

Directions: Take the A52 from Skegness. Go over the bridge crossing the river and turn right, fishing is on this bank only.

Description: This part of the river produces excellent fishing in both the winter and summer months. The perch are a good size and the the roach are in abundance. In the summer the bream and tench can reach over 5lbs.
The downside is that in places this section of river is very shallow at only 2 feet. There are plenty of platforms making access easy for the disabled angler.
Lastly there are some big pike that hunt in the edges. This can be the reason it goes quite for a while.

Types of Fish: Bream, tench, perch, pike, roach.

Rules/Bans: No joker or bloodworm

Facilities: Parking at the riverside. Disabled access.

P   ♿   68

Telephone: Skegness Fishing Tackle 01754 611172

River Glen
Pinchbeck.

Ticket Price: Day ticket £3.00 on the bank.

Directions: From Surfleet to Pinchbeck use the footpath on the south bank. The B1180 runs alongside the south bank of the river between Pinchbeck and West Pinchbeck.

Description: This non-tidal navigation of 11.5 miles begins at Tongue End, near Bourne and passes through several villages before merging with the River Welland at Surfleet Seas End.

Types of Fish: Bream, roach, perch, pike and eel.

Rules/Bans: Not known.

Facilities: Road side parking.

P

69

Telephone: 01775 723451 Spalding Fishing Club

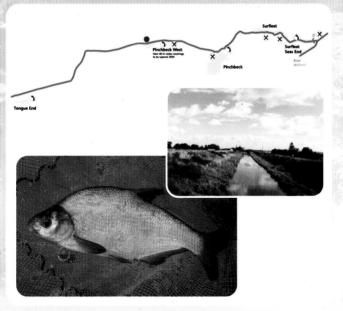

Lincolnshire Drains

The area covered is basically between Boston and the Lincolnshire Wolds and takes in waters under the control of Boston & District Angling Association and the Witham & District Joint Angling Federation.

Starting with the **Hobhole Drain**. This runs to the right and parallel with the A16 from just south of the small town of Spilsby to its outfall into the Haven to the east of Boston. This serves all of that eastern area to the coast via smaller (fishable) drains such as the Bellwater and Fodderdyke and even some across to its west side. The water is effectively split into two halfway along its length at the Lade Bank pumping station, above which control is vested in the New Leake AC, and below with the Boston & District A.A. The width ranges from approx 12 metres at its northern end to around 25 metres and more towards the outfall, with depths in the 1.5 – 3 metre category. Most of the water from the

HOBHOLE DRAIN

top end down to the main road bridge (A52) at Halltoft End has roadside access on the eastern side as well as walking in on the opposite bank from the various bridges. Below that there are vehicular accessible tracks on the eastern side between the Clampgate and Nunn's Bridges, right down to the outfall pumping station. Care should be taken in most areas, particularly on the eastern bank where the water is quite some way down from the top of the bank which is also very steep. Taking the water as a whole the drain sports a fair number of bream shoals which include huge specimens to 8lbs and can give both match and pleasure anglers nets of 50lbs and much more, as recent NFA national winners can vouch for.

Roach and perch and some hybrid's are not in abundance during the summer but are generally in the 4- 8oz range in the case of the roach, whilst the perch can turn up in any swim, particularly when pleasure fishing, and can be as much as 2lbs and more.

Whilst feeding into this same drain at Freiston Doors Bridge, the **Cowbridge Drain** in actual fact serves land to the West of the A16 and even the Sibsey Trader Drain and has an unusual feature in that it crosses under that drain at Cowbridge without any direct connection to it. Most of this water is accessed by the north bank from the Bakers to Kelsey bridge, after which it is really only walking from there or the Boston Golf Course. Much the same sort of species, and more in the way of smaller fish, plus a decent head of tench to liven things up during the summer months. Also a couple of bream shoals along this two mile length and seven anglers in a line took weights between 7 and 14KGs in last years national.

Locks at the golf course separate this watercourse from the **West Fen Drain** which serves the whole of the north west area with the Rivers Witham and Bain on its west and north boundaries respectively. In effect the system has a double arm as the Frith Bank Drain which is locked to the Witham at Antons Gowt also

WEST FEN DRAIN

goes around in a wide arc to join up with its sister towards the tiny village of Bunkers Hill. This water is really only fished for the resident bream shoal at the golf course end during the summer months but comes into its own over the winter period in Frithville village where roach nets to 30lbs or more can be achieved when conditions are favourable.

This brings us to the **Sibsey Trader Drain** system which can be traced from its outfall into the Haven in the middle of Boston right through to the edge of the Wolds to the north some 10 miles hence. Starting from the outfall, the water comes in different guises and from there to Bargate Bridge is known as, logically, the **Bargate Drain** with 70 permanent pegs. The vast majority of these are easily accessed along a footpath with the main parking on Windsor Crescent. This section usually holds a huge population of small roach, perch and skimmers during the summer months together with a fair head of good bream and tench to 5lbs.The other side of the bridge brings you immediately to Maud Foster Mill and so not unnaturally is known as the **Maud Foster Drain** from there to Cowbridge and covers approximately 100 fishable pegs in a drain width of around twenty two metres and depths in the 5 – 6 ft range.

It perhaps contains less in the way of small fish but a bigger

BARGATE DRAIN

head of those bream and tench, which talking of the latter, can turn up in any swim and fre- quently do. This drain now boasts a good fishing platform at every peg from the outfall at Mount Bridge to a little way short of Cowbridge, around 150 in total. The **Sibsey Trader Drain** itself starts immediately from Cowbridge and continues northwards on the left side of, and parallel to the A16 for some six miles to the village of Sibsey Northlands. Here it splits at Cherry Corner into the East & West Fen Catchwaters, which are in the main unfishable during summer months for too much weed growth and have low water levels during winter (on a normal dry year).

This water is around 20 metres wide, being 5-6 ft in depth and contains a good head of roach, perch, skimmers and large bream but is something of an enigma as small club matches invariably struggle for decent weights on a weekend.

Pleasure fishing and big matches on the other hand usually bring out some super nets of roach, skimmers and those big bream, as can be seen from previous national events. Roadside access is available from the golf course to Northlands Bridge, around 300 pegs, but currently some sections are out of bounds due to regulations on overhead power cables which may be reviewed during this close season.

SILSEY TRADER DRAIN

The main waterway is the **River Witham** which is much wider and deeper than any other in the area. Also much longer than most realise, starting as it does near S. Witham on the Lincolnshire border with Rutland County. From there it wends its way northwards taking in Grantham and Lincoln before taking a sharp right turn in the city to run down to Boston, some 70 miles or so in total. Not much more than a large delph or beck as it goes from Grantham to Lincoln but certainly in the Long Benington and Claypole area contains many specimen fish of the usual species but also hold many good chub and barbel to spice up proceedings for the pleasure angler. The first named area is controlled by Grantham & DAA whilst the Claypole section comes under Newark & District Piscatorial. Heading into the Lincoln approaches, the water gradually widens and deepens to hold good shoals of roach, perch and bream within the city limits and is administered by Lincoln & District AA. On to the eastern side of the city it now enlarges dramatically to take in the summer boat traffic which uses the waterway to get from the Midlands via the R.Trent and the Fossdyke Canal to access the east coast at Boston. Unfortunately this part of river suffers too much weed in the summer months and is only easy accessible from the various bridges along its 30 mile length. Most of the water comes under the jurisdiction of the Witham & District joint Angling Federation whose jewel in the crown is a small stretch some 4 miles from the Kirkstead to Tattershall bridges through to Chapel Hill, having roadside access. The river is on average 30 or more metres wide and apart from its renowned bream shoals has little else to attract the pleasure angler as roach and skimmers are too thin on the ground during those summer months. A different story for the winter period as these same fish shoal up in a few pegs at the previously mentioned bridges when water levels are well down.

SOUTH FORTY FOOT DRAIN

Swinging round now to the west and south of Boston, and to the other side of the R. Witham, is another extensive drainage system in the shape of the **South & North Forty Foot Drains**. The South Forty Foot is the main drain which is locked in Boston into the Haven.

This is fed by other much smaller drains including the N. Forty Foot along its entire length, which in total cover a large area of land in a sickle shape going right round to the R. Glen beyond Bourne and to the south of Spalding. Also a little under stocked and suffering from lack of access apart from bridges, nearly all of those smaller drains have pumping stations at their outfall into the main water, effectively preventing any natural fish movement between the two over the course of a year. It does boast some bream but most anglers tackle the venue with roach, perch and skimmers in mind and certainly the Boston end contains its fair share of these during the summer, given that the drain does not suffer salt ingress on a very dry year. Similarly for the N. Forty Foot drain which has good roadside access within Boston as well as around five miles beyond the B1192 towards Holland Fen. Unfortunately this drain, although containing a good variety of fish, does suffer from steep banks and an abundance of summer weed and is hardly a choice for local anglers who tend to choose more amenable facilities – spoilt for choice in other words! Finally to the south of the county in the Spalding region which also boasts a myriad of drains, many of which are administered by the East Midlands Angling Federation, of which Boston & D.A.A. are a part. The **Coronation Channel** and **Vernatts Drain** are the main waters in and around Spalding town itself. The former is generally at its best during those summer months although access is again limited to bridges. Both waters do contain shoals of bream as well as the occasional tench but also retain an angler's interest with good populations of roach, perch and skimmers. All in all a Boston & D.A.A. book holder has a wealth of waters to go at, and belonging to the other mentioned angling bodies, has access to well over 100 miles of water from the Fossdyke Canal and R. Witham in the north and west, to the Hobhole Drain and Coronation Channel in the east and south.

Ticket Price: Day tickets £3.00. Annual book £15.00. Concessionary annual book £11.00.

Types of Fish: Roach, perch, tench and bream.

Rules/Bans: No bloodworm or joker.

Telephone: To book pegs and match booking ring 01205 871815

70

Information kindly supplied by Barbara Clifton and Barry Mallett of the Boston & District Angling Association.

Three Rivers (Drains)
Pilfrey Bridge, Althorpe.

Ticket Price: Day tickets £3.50 on the bank.
Season Tickets £15.00.

Directions: Take the A18 from Scunthorpe heading west. Drive through Gunness and continue through Althorpe. As soon as you pass over the first drain (Pilfrey Bridge) turn right into the car park.

Description: The River Torne passes close to Three Rivers which are made up of three parallel running drains (not rivers) that are connected which therefore have the same species in each. Most popular is the Middle Drain, which I believe is the deepest. Tench and bream are the fish to target both of which reach 7lbs, (try sweet corn). There's plenty of roach that go for maggot or caster.

Types of Fish: Quality roach to 2lbs, large perch, bream and tench to 7lbs, pike to 25lbs + eels around 2lbs.

Rules/Bans: None

Number of Lakes: Three drains

Facilities: Car parking.

Telephone: Scunthorpe DAA 01652 655849

83

T A C K L E   S H O P S

Alvingham Fisheries, Lock Rd, Alvingham, Louth, LN11 7EU. 01507 328271

Baitline International, Littlefield Lane, Marsh Chapel, Grimsby N.E. Lincs, DN36 5TJ. 01472 388800

Barry's of Goole Ltd, 25 Westfield Avenue, Goole, N Lincs, DN14 6JY. 01405 762869

Boston Angling Centre, 11 Horncastle Rd, Boston, PE21 9BN. 01205 353436

Castaline, 18-20 Upgate, Louth, Lincolnshire, LN11 9ET. 01507 602149

Castaway Tackle, Unit 8b, Chieftain Way, Tritton Rd Trading Estate, Lincoln, LN6 7RY. 01522 567090

Change Coarse Ltd, Unit 5-7 Wetherby Crescent, Lincoln, Lincolnshire, LN6 8SX. 01522 690031

Chapel Tackle. 7 The Green, Chapel St. Leonards PE24 5TH. 01754 87165   01754 87165

Chapmans Sea & Game, 29 Beechway, Scunthorpe, N.E. Lincolnshire, DN16 2HF. 01724 277551

Chapmans Specialist Tackle, 23-29, Beechway, Scunthorpe, Lincolnshire, DN16 2HF. 01724 858982

Cleethorpes Angling Centre, 291 Brereton Avenue, Cleethorpes, Lincs DN35 7QX. 01472 602002

Cleethorpes Tight Lines, 51 Cambridge St, Cleethorpes, Lincolnshire, DN35 8HD. 01472 322206

Country Lines, Bridge Street, Brigg DN20 8NW. 01652 651650 01652 651650

Daves Peg, 1 London Rd, Sleaford, Lincolnshire, NG34 7LF. 01529 415896

David's Tackle, 91 High St, Heckington, Sleaford, Lincolnshire, NG34 9QU. 01529 460330

FBT, Unit 7 Station Estate, Newbridge Hill, Louth, Lincolnshire, LN11 0JT. 01507 601774

Fred's Fishing Tackle, 413 Weelsby St, Grimsby, N.E. Lincolnshire, DN32 8BJ. 01472 352922

Geds Fenland Tackle, 49 Hallgate, Holbeach, Spalding, PE12 7JA. 01406 422020

G Harrison & Son, 55 Croft St, Lincoln, Lincolnshire, LN2 5AZ. 01522 523834

Granz Angling, 25 New Rd, Spaulding PE11 1DQ. 01775 712206

Hatfield R.A, 125 Rowland Rd, Scunthorpe, N.E. Lincolnshire, DN16 1TQ. 01724 861786

Holbeach Angling, 18 Church St, Holbeach, Spaulding. 01406 420444

Hooked, 44 High St, Boston, Lincolnshire, PE21 8SP. 01205 355655

Humberside Angling Centre, 63-67 Pasture St, Grimsby, Lincolnshire, DN32 9AB. 01472 322300

Kingfisher Tackle Shop, 37 Fleetgate, Barton-Upon-Humber, Lincolnshire, DN18 5QA. 01652 636868

K.W Storr, 37/38 High St, Wainfleet, Skegness, Lincolnshire, PE24 4BJ. 01754 880378

Lightwoods of Grimsby, 172, Cleethorpe Rd, Grimsby, N.E. Lincolnshire, DN31 3HW. 01472 343536

Newport Tackle Shop, 85 Newport, Lincoln, Lincolnshire, LN1 3DW. 01522 525861

Oham Lake, Oham Main Rd, Maltby-le-Marsh, Alford, Lincolnshire, LN13 0JP. 01507 450623

Riverside Tackle, Tattershall Bridge, Lincoln, Lincolnshire, LN4 4JW. 01526 344660

R.S Tackle & Guns, Unit 1, Carlisle St, Goole, North Lincolnshire, DN14 5DS. 01405 720292

Rutland Fishing, 7 St. Pauls St, Stamford, Lincolnshire, PE9 2BE. 01780 482901

Short Ferry Angling, Ferry Road, Fiskerton, LIncoln LN3 4HU. 01526 398021 01526 398102

Skegness Fishing Tackle, 155/157 Roman Bank, Skegness, Lincolnshire, PE25 1RY. 01754 611172

Slingsbys, 19 Westgate, Sleaford, Lincolnshire, NG34 7PJ. 01529 302836

South End Angling, 447 High St, Lincoln, Lincolnshire, LN5 8HZ. 01522 528627

Sparks Bros, 43 Cromwell Avenue, Grimsby, N.E. Lincolnshire, DN31 2DR. 01472 342613

Scunthorpe Fishing Tackle Centre, 9 Laneham St, Scunthorpe, Lincolnshire, DN15 6LJ. 01724 849815

Stamford Tackle, 13a Foundry Rd, Stamford, PE9 2PY. 01780 754541

Storrs, 37-38 High St, Wainfleet, Skegness, PE24 4BJ. 01754 880378

Tackle 4U, 155 Roman Bank, Skegness. PE25 1RY. 01754 611172

Tackle 4U, Skegness Rd Ingoldmells, Skegness, PE25 1NP. 01754 874950

The Anglers Workshop, Unit 3, Haven Mill, Garth Lane, Grimsby, Lincolnshire, DN3. 01472 351125

The Tackle Shop, Bridge Rd, Gainsborough, Lincolnshire, DN21 1JU. 01427 613002

Tidswell Tackle, New Bungalow, Burr Lane, Spalding, Lincolnshire. 01775 723640

Tight Lines. 51 Cambridge Street, Cleethorpes DN35 8HD. 01472 200400 01472 200400

Tight Line Services, 55 Croft St, Lincoln, Lincolnshire, LN2 5AZ. 01522 569555

Vanguard Fishing Tackle, 2 Midland Buildings, Skegness Rd, Ingoldmells, PE25 1NP. 01754 874950

Vanguard Fishing Tackle Ltd, 25 Wide Bargate, Boston, Lincolnshire, PE21 6SR. 01205 369994

Vanguard Fishing Tackle Ltd, 155 Roman Bank, Skegness. 01754 611172

Whisby Angling Supplies, Unit 6, Exchange Rd, Lincoln, LN6 3JZ. 01522 684464

Woodlands Tackle Shop, Ashby Rd, Spilsby, PE23 5DW. 01790 754252

I N D E X

If you know of a fishery that is not included in this guide or you want to update an existing venue. Please fill in the form below.

Fishery Name

Fishery Address

Post code

Contact Name

Telephone No

| Adult Day Ticket Price | £ | concession OAP'S | £ |

Fish species and approximate weights

Brief Description

Rules / Bans

Facilities

Number of Lakes

Please e-mail or post a colour photo for inclusion in the next publication.

Please return this form to:
Fish-it
Pickard Communication
10-11 Riverside Park,
Sheaf Gardens,
Sheffield S2 4BB.
Fax: (0114) 275 8866

New Fishery ☐

Update to Fishery ☐

New Fishery / Fishery Update Form

Notes